The Ramblings of A Crazy Lady

I0117212

Dawn Pritchard

chipmunkapublishing
the mental health publisher

Published by

Chipmunkapublishing

PO Box 6872

Brentwood

Essex CM13 1ZT

United Kingdom

http://www.chipmunkapublishing.com

Copyright © Dawn Pritchard 2012

ISBN   978-1-84747-930-3

Chipmunkapublishing gratefully acknowledge the support of Arts Council England.

Biography

Born in 1973 Dawn Pritchard was brought up in Leeds. She has one younger sister. She now lives in Hertfordshire with Lesley, her partner of ten years. Dawn qualified as a Social Worker in July 2000. Following an overdose in 2001 she was diagnosed with Borderline Personality Disorder. Over the past ten years she has written a number of poems about her experiences, treatment, therapy, hospital admissions, suicide attempts, and periods of self-harm. She only ever shared a few of her poems with certain family and trusted professionals, as she never believed anyone else would understand or identify with it. Was she right?

Eleven years ago following an overdose my mum gave me a plain paged book, this is what she wrote on the first page. It was in that book that I began writing my poetry.

To my dear Daughter,

This is the first day of the rest of your life.
Use this book as you need to, good days, bad days, sad and happy, your thoughts and feelings.
The only thing I ask is be honest and true.
There will come a time when you won't need this book.
Love from your Mum
xxx

August 18th 2001

This book is for anyone who has ever thought, it must just be me.

It's not and you're not alone

Acknowledgements

For all their love, support, encouragement and humour over the years, I would like to thank my soul mate Lesley, my sister Adele, my 'nephew' Georgia and my very good friend Sam. I love you all.

To mum and dad, I love you both very much

A very big thank you goes to Laura May, for her help in putting the collection together.

Poem

The light's gone out, there's no one home
I'm sitting here, all alone,
Staring out, into space
I close my eyes, and see your face

You look at me like nothing's wrong
I open my eyes but you are gone
I lie in bed awake each night
Wondering if what I did was right

The pain it never seems to stop
It's like an endless ticking clock
Reminding me of times gone by
I curl into a ball and cry

I rack my brain for things to do
Things that don't remind me of you
I wish I'd never left you now
Could we have stayed together, not sure how

Everywhere I seem to go
There's a little piece of you you know
Sitting on my shoulder, inside my head
It really hurts so much I wish that I was dead

2.30am

It's 2.30 in the morning and I'm wide awake in bed
Wondering what the hell it is that's racing
through my head
The thoughts they seem so many, it's difficult to see
I once again conclude, it simply must be me

When will it all just stop, when will it let me be
These thoughts they drive me crazy, when will
my mind be free
I just want to close my eyes, and gently fall asleep
But, no my mind keeps racing, it will not let me sleep

Dawn Pritchard

The Darkness

I close my eyes
Shut out the light
I fall into the darkness

I close my ears
Shut out the sound
I fall into the darkness

My thoughts they drift
They fade away
I fall into the darkness

My heart it beats
So very slow
I fall into the darkness

My body sinks
Into the bed
I fall into the darkness

No hurt, no pain
No fear again
I fall into the darkness

This is my death
Take my last breath
I fall into the darkness

I feel no guilt
I feel no shame
For I will be reborn again

For I am the darkness

My Shrink

Can someone please explain to me
Why my psychiatrist seems to be
So hell bent on confusing me

He tells me that I'm playing games,
For which there seem to be no names
Just leaves me feeling guilt and shame

For him it must be alright
I guess he doesn't lie awake at night
Wondering what's wrong, what's right,

Can't he see I find it tough,
My life it sometimes feels so rough
And all he does is huff n puff

He seems to think I enjoy being like this
Feeling like I don't exist
He really sometimes takes the piss

Can someone please explain to me,
Why my psychiatrist seems to be
So hell bent on confusing me

Dawn Pritchard

Therapy

I'm sat in a corner inside my head

Nothing to say - everything has been said

I sit all alone, curled up in a ball

No matter what people say, I'll never walk tall

The darkness inside me, is slowly eating away

At my very existence, I'll disappear one day

I try to climb out, but always seem to fall

There doesn't seem to be anyone who can hear me call

I want to feel normal, and get on with my life

But the pain it cuts deep, it's as sharp as a knife

There's a glimmer of light, I run towards it full speed

Will this provide the help I so greatly need.

You will see

What am I supposed to do
When I just can't get through to you
The things I do, the things I say
Will all make sense to you one day

When my body turns to dust
In my words you'll begin to trust
For that is when you will see
That life begins in death for me

No more fear, no more pain
I get to live my life again
You'll look back and try to see
What you could've done for me

Eventually you will agree
I did what I did
So I could be free

Dawn Pritchard

The three that make me

I'm sitting here wondering why
The child within, must die
The pain is too much, we can't take anymore
Just take loads of tablets then she'll be no more

We just want it to stop, want it all to end
The arguments, the conflict, drive us round the bend
Fred is clever, wants to be in control
But Dippy feels that this is her role

Don't let Pebbles talk she'll ruin it all
Just put her to sleep, so she can't hear the call
Cut out the bad bits and throw them away
Through death you will see it's the only way

Permanent sleep is the answer we seek
Pebbles' holds all the emotions and that
makes her weak
Pick yourself up, and sort yourself out
Behave, eat your dinner, then they'll let you out

Let Dippy take over, she'll talk to them right
They'll see she's calm and sensible, then they'll
let her out
You don't need to be here, you're wasting their time
Why do people see suicide as a crime

If this is my life why can't we choose
Just curl up in a ball and have that long snooze
You can't turn us off we are here to stay
You have to listen to what we say

Find a nice quiet place, no chaos, no stress
Take blades and tablets, equals permanent rest.

Yesterday

I watch the clouds floating by
High up in the clear blue sky
I sometimes wish that I could too
Float away and disperse as they do

Yesterday I felt such pain
But today I've hidden it once again
The shutters they come down by themselves
And I'm trapped again in a living hell

Why can't I say what needs to be said
Why does it feel like I'm better off dead
The switch is flicked once again
And the emotions and pain retreat to their den

Why can't I reach them, why can't I say
What really happened on that Boxing Day
Pebbles, the child that lives deep within
Is really terrified to let anyone in

Will someone please help me let Pebbles speak
I can't do it alone, the journey's too steep
I don't want to spend my life just running away
Pebbles she has so much to say

Help me remember and get things straight
I can't spend my whole life full of fear and hate
Help me look after her, give her some care
The others have had their turn, it's only fair

Pretend

17 years ago pebbles was born
To take care of our soul that was damaged and torn
She cried into her pillow night after night
Scared to tell anyone of her plight

The following morning after the damage was done
She felt to embarrassed and afraid to tell anyone
She tried to pretend it didn't happen at all
And so Pebbles' voice became very small

Even when we went for the HIV test
We didn't tell anyone, we thought it was best
Pebbles has lived in the shadows, up until now
But where should she start, we just don't know how

The images and flashbacks are still in our head
The pain becomes too much, we wish we were dead
Where do you start with something that hurts so much
Because we start to detach and then we lose touch

We tell it as a story with no connection to me
But we know we must own it to set ourselves free
Our memory is hazy of what happened you see
So we try to pretend, it didn't happen to me

You labelled me

I woke this morning in a state
Thinking of Dr T and Cate
Wondering why he always said no
On the ward I must never go

He labelled me with BPD
But never explored the impact on me
Just told me that I was playing games
For which there seemed to be no names

Then suddenly in a flash of light
Told me I was cured almost over night
Now Dr Smith has told me
I most definitely still have BPD

Is it any wonder I feel so confused
My head feels like it's been used and abused
For me truth and honesty is a must
Who do I listen to, who do I trust

I realise I can't go on like this
Feeling like I don't exist
Lost and trapped in my own mind
Taking overdoses hoping they don't find

The chaos has gone there's a peaceful calm
My mind is focused with thoughts of self harm
If I was to end my life today
Not sure how I'd do it, but there would be a way

Why do I think I'd be better off dead?
Because I can't cope with the emotions inside my head
Feelings and emotions they hurt too much
Physical pain you can see and can touch

Dawn Pritchard

Demons

I'm laid here on my bed
Mulling over what's been said
The voices seem so quiet now
Not telling me what to do, or how

I wonder if they will return
Shouting at me out of turn
They have been here for so long
My head feels empty now they've gone

I know they made me do dangerous stuff
But they were always there when things got tough
Helped me get through the darkest days
Even though I hurt myself in various ways

Now I wonder how I will cope
When things go wrong and it feels like there's no hope
Will I reach for pills and blades
Fred decides when these decisions are made

Although I have come so far
My thoughts wander back to sitting in the car
Cutting myself to see the blood
Try taking my life, I know I could

I'm so terrified of the feelings inside
I just want to disappear and hide
The genie has been let out of the bottle you see
And I'm left trying to find the real me

How do I cope, what will I do
Will the plans of my past eventually come true
Take myself off, just hide away
They won't find me until the next day

How do you fight demons, that hurt so much
When they've hidden away, from kind human touch
Sat in the corner, they're waiting to pounce
They take all my strength, every single ounce

It's only a shell

Why can't they see, my life will begin when I am dead
I should've realised, they couldn't get it
through their heads
By killing the shell that they know as Dawn
This will enable us to be reborn

Death isn't the end it's the beginning you see
By ending it all, it will set us all free
Pebbles can become a person in her own right
It'll stop all the pain and having to fight

The tablets just numb us they don't stop the pain
We just want our freedom to live once again
Tell Les that you love her, then say our goodbyes
Don't turn around because we'll see her cry

I know she'll be angry and upset at first
But living with us like this, has got to be worse
The mood swings, the self-harm
She deserves peace and calm

To die is to free oneself of pain
It's a new beginning, start over again
This body we carry is a physical shell
Walking around in this living hell

On the Ward

When I'm asleep, it stops the voices in my head
But when I wake up I wish I was dead
Tell Pebbles to stop crying and sharing her pain
Fred will take over and protect her again

Cut out the hurt bits, throw them away
We'll die soon, maybe today
The pain cuts so deep as sharp as a knife
The only way to stop it is by taking our life

Head straight for the darkness, run at it full speed
The darkness will give us, the strength that we need
The tablets are trying to drown out our voice
Don't let them take hold and remove our choice

I'm scared of the emotions and feelings that lie within
If you tell them the truth they'll just keep you in
Just close your eyes, squeeze them really tight
And maybe, we will die in the night

Cut open your arm and watch the blood flow
Death this way, will be really slow
As life begins to slowly slip away
We will be, reborn some day

Keep looking around for something to use
Plastic knife, spoon or can, we can then choose
They doctors they just don't understand
We are just, not meant for this land

Crying doesn't help us, just makes us feel sad
Frustrates us and angers us, makes us go mad
So tell them you're okay, now you feel fine
Then off somewhere quiet, just take our time.

Dawn Pritchard

On Obs

They're watching us now, everything that we do
It's all Fred's fault, now they're watching us too
You think you're so clever, storming off in a craze
Now they won't let us leave, for many more days

We shouldn't have agreed, to come in in the first place
Because now they're watching us just in case
Should have taken more tablets, so that
we did not wake
Just would've been better for everyone's sake

The thoughts are still there they won't go away
It's now just a case, of picking the day
Got to be careful, make sure the timing is right
Maybe we should do it in the middle of the night

Plotting and planning what can we do
Not a great deal whilst they're watching you
Stay calm and settled and just do not say
That we've made up our mind that today is the day

How can they be wrong?

Pebbles' wants to scream and shout
She desperately wants to let it all out
The problem is she doesn't know where to start
Because a long time ago someone tore her apart

The pain cuts deep and sharp like a knife
Please someone help her before we end her life
Fred wants to end it, take it away
The thoughts are so strong and are there everyday

The overdose was meant to put us to sleep
We're trying to keep promises we know we can't keep
Find things and hide them, don't tell them where
Use them secretly so no-one's aware

These feelings won't stop until we are dead
Keep them locked up inside your head
Hang yourself, cut yourself, jump from a building up high
Our spirit will live on and float in the sky

Tell Les that you love her, then just slip away
Mum, Dad we're sorry, but it's the only way
I know they'll be sad and upset that you've gone
But the thoughts are so strong, how can they be wrong?

Dawn Pritchard

That little girl is me

Once upon a time, not too long ago
There was a little girl who just did not know
That all the pain she felt inside
Was why she'd run away and hide

Being hurt at a young age
The others locked her in a cage
She searched around to find the key
And now I've realised that little girl is me

How do I talk to her, what do I say
How do I help her, and in what way
That little girl is, so scared you see
What do I do to set her free

The door's now open, and she wants to step out
But the others start to scream and shout
Telling her she shouldn't speak
Because telling people makes us weak

We can tell a story about someone else
But we cannot own it for ourself
The little girl she wants to say
What happened to her on that Boxing Day

You're Gone

It's been four weeks today

And there's still no words to say

That will ever take the pain away

The fact that you're gone

Is so very, very wrong

I don't want to be strong

Just knowing you're not here

Brings on floods of tears

I wish that you were near

In my thoughts is where you'll stay

Until we meet again, and I can say

I love you Aunty Jacqui forever and always

Dawn Pritchard

When will I be free?

It's 1.30 in the morning
And I'm wide awake in bed
Trying to focus on the thoughts
That are racing through my head

They fly by so quickly
It's so difficult to see
Attach any meaning
Of what they mean to me

I've spent my life just running
Trying to avoid my past
But my demons they run faster
They've caught up with me at last

Trying to attach feelings
To something that has no name
My mind feels invaded
I don't want to feel the pain

I know this is the process
I know this is what I've got to do
But I'm terrified of the journey
And whether I'll make it through

Soon it will be morning
And reality starts again
So stop my mind from racing
Else I'll drive myself insane

Pick up where we left off
One session to another
You try tap into my feelings
And I run for the covers

When will I stop avoiding
The being that is me
When will I stop running
When will I be free

Dawn Pritchard

To Blame

I'm sitting here wondering why
I find it so hard to open up and cry
To grieve for all that I have lost
No, must keep it in at any cost

The part of me that died that night
Didn't even put up a fight
Just left that room feeling guilt and shame
But knowing nothing would be the same

Feeling lost and so confused
Physical pain from being used
Kept it to myself, let no-one see
What my own stupidity did to me

You see I think I'm still to blame
Challenged my mum to a drinking game
If only I had done things right
I might not have suffered loss that night

Alphabet of Feelings

What is this inside of me
Bubbling up, wanting to be free
Their faces look so full of pain
The trauma of the hurt again

Sadness, loneliness lots of shame
These feelings tell me they have names
Pain and loss, try pushing through
Anger and rage, I think they're here too

So the alphabet of feelings has been living in my head
Gathering momentum feeling like it's made of lead
So the haziness is not a cold, just old stories left untold
Buried deep like they were gold

To the surface they must come
But slowly, slowly one by one
Emotions can be high and flat
Too many at once and you best call CATT

So will these feelings set me free
Let my mind and soul just be
Will releasing these emotions from my past
Give me the closure I need, at last

Dawn Pritchard

Why should I value me?

Why should I value me?
There is no worth that I can see
Never been quite good enough
Didn't make the grade, well that's just tough

Do you know, I took 8 GCSE's
Got 6 with grades A to C
Thought it would make my father pleased
"You'll end up stacking shelves", is all he teased

When I took my A Level exams
Off to uni was the plan
But I didn't quite get the grades
So at my parents I just stayed

Started drinking every night
Really to just block out the shite
The shite was emotions and feelings you see
And I didn't know how to handle these

Even though I used to go out with mum
And we used to have lots of fun
She was now more like a friend
The mum n daughter thing was at an end

My dad was always a hero to me
I was convinced he loved me unconditionally
That was until I told him I was gay
I think I broke his heart that day

You see this is why I feel so bad
I make my parents really sad
So why should I value me
There is no worth that I can see

Poem

It feels like the end is near

No more heart ache, no more tears

No more time to sit a wallow

No more feeling numb and hollow

This is where the journey starts

I know it's gonna break some hearts

But time's a healer, so they say

They'll get over it some day

I cannot go on, living in such pain

It will drive me totally insane

Not trusting what's inside my head

I really rather would be dead

Dawn Pritchard

Endings

Writing this was so extremely tough
I knew the words just wouldn't be enough
You see the things I'd like to say
Would probably take a year and a day

So I present you with this model, yeah I know
it's a little bit weird
No I'm not an anorak yet, as the doctors had first feared
It's a metaphorical representation of our therapeutic
journey together
No it's not, it's tons of matches, and days of PVA
sticking my fingers together

Though the fact it is a merry-go-round, really is quite apt
The ups n downs, the round n round, the trying to adapt
Therapy's been quite like that, first trusting to
get on the horse
Especially knowing I'd probably fall off as
a matter of course

The ride it has been painful, essential and confusing too
But your approach, technique, personality or whatever
it is you do
Really deserves respect, cos you helped
me to get through
But the working in your socks, maybe you need
some help too

Anyway, each individual match was measured, cut,
glued and sanded by hand
I had to follow instructions, an architect
wouldn't understand
Stephen I know you get this, you know what
I'm trying to say
But the words themselves at the moment are
just too painful to say.

So please accept this gift as my way to say
I really do wish you weren't leaving today

Dawn Pritchard

Not too deep

Find a blade nice and thin

Plunge it into your unbroken skin

Cut a line not too deep

The emotions will begin to seep

They're coming through my skin and pores

We know the reason, we know the cause

See the blood running red

These are the words never said

I do not want to take my life

I want no trouble, no more strife

Try and let the emotions free

Will that bring peace, let me be

Help

All I ever did was try to please
But you just taunted and just teased
We'd play fight, but you'd get rough
I'd get upset and you'd say tough

I always thought you wanted a little boy
But I was born a girl, and I was not a toy
You'd turn out the lights and make me scared
I'd scream and shout, but you never cared

I looked up to you, needed your help
But like a puppy you watched me yelp
What did I do, to make you act this way
Laughed at and dismissed, never really had my say

I still look up to you, you know, desperate for you to see
You are the main man in my life, you mean the
world to me
I try so hard to fit in, leave my emotions at the door
But you ignore me, don't see me, that rocks
me to my core

Another man hurt me, took what wasn't his
But you deny it happened, claiming I would've
told you this
How could I have told you, when I didn't have a voice
Try deny it happened, was my only choice

Anger

Why can't I be angry at those who have hurt me

I run from my emotions, desperate to break free

Anger feels so bad, like it's not allowed

If I were to release it, it would destroy an entire crowd

Who do I aim it at, how do I let it go

The smile you see upon my face, really is just for show

You see inside I'm raging, the anger it wants out

But I'm too frightened to raise my voice, let alone shout

Emotional Games

Why did you hurt me

Couldn't you see

The games you were playing

Really hurt me

I was just a little girl

Wanting to fit in

When I told you I was gay

It was like I'd committed some kind of sin

Emotional tennis was your game

And I was the ball

Batted between you to and fro

Never picked up when I'd fall

You'd say you were getting divorced again

As I got up for school in the morning

This would be on my mind all day

Not knowing if you'd be home, when I got in

Dawn Pritchard

The Drone on the phone

I'm sat in my office, it's quite late at night
Feeling both physically n mentally quite shite
I knew once you left, just what they'd do
Dropped like a hot potato right on cue

Support is forthcoming I was told over the phone
Watford will be my saviours, I was told by the drone
But in the meantime, I can give duty a call
So long as I don't want, to talk about feelings at all

You see I tried to explain, the situation with my mum
And the drone on the phone was confused
by this conundrum
Why would she be like that he asks of me
I said mate if I knew that, my mind would be free

He said Dawn you really must try computerised CBT
I said I've tried it, it didn't work it's not for me
I really was beginning to get pissed off with this call
So I told him straight, mate it's not one size fits all

After this challenge the drone needed a break
Because he decided his leave of this call he would take
Take care Dawn he said as he put down the phone
Don't forget you can call duty if you need a drone

Integration

Let the little people have a voice
Give them options, let them make a choice
Do they want to live alone
Or integrate and become one

See now that depends on who you ask
For some it's not a simple task
Giving over all they know
With nothing left to show

What happens to them, when they're gone?
Does it mean all they held was simply wrong
If the new way forward is not their way
Will they no longer have a say

When 3 become 2, then 2 become 1
Does it mean all their work has been undone
Integration! What does it really mean?
No longer heard, no longer seen

Will we exist in the background
Waiting for intros, like scraps off the ground
You don't seem to understand
We were your gong, your marching band

We held you up, we made our stand
It was us who held your hand

Dawn Pritchard

Poem

One step at a time

Easier said than done

Try lay down and get some sleep

We're not here for the fun

You pushed for us to be here

But now, you've not said a word

Frightened of the consequences

Should your voice be heard

Don't you see that is the point

It's time for her to speak

Time to tell the world

Let them hear she's not a freak

She's just a little girl

Who was never shown the way

Your journey now starts here

We can help you on your way

That Night

Once upon, some time ago
A little girl, I know said no
But sadly, she was not listened to
So I'll tell you about what she went through

Pebbles was this young girls' name
And from that night she wasn't the same
She felt unable to scream and fight
And had no support to share her plight

Feeling embarrassed and full of shame
She didn't even know his name
What could she do, who could she tell
Her life turned into a living hell

She stills sees herself upon that floor
And remembers kissing him at the door
But she didn't say, let's go all the way
She just wouldn't, she was still a virgin on that day

She said she'd scream if he didn't stop
But he just continued, laid on top
She put her hands down below
How long she'd been there, she didn't know

She could feel him, pushing inside
She told to stop, she really tried
She really didn't want to be there
But he wasn't bothered, he didn't care

When he finished he got up and left
She just lay there, half undressed
Scared and frightened, what should she do
No-one would believe her if she told the truth

Back down to the party Pebbles went
He asked for a kiss, offered a drink like a gent
Confused and hurt she walked away
But who could she tell, what would she say

In the morning, when she woke
She hoped it had been some kind of joke
But when she tried to have a pee
It hurt so much, and there was blood you see

Deep inside she knew what he'd done
But what could she do, where could she run
She knew she'd been drinking and would be blamed
So deny it happened, hide the shame

Battle

There's a battle going on, inside my head
The voices are saying we'll end up dead
They can no longer exist within the same space
Neither one backing down, neither wants to lose face

The words now are out there and we can't
take them back
The tears come flooding along with the flashbacks
How can I explain to them, there's no longer any
sense to their fight
They were all created from the same victim, when
I was raped that night

They've served their purpose well, the defences I've
picked up on the way
But deep inside always knowing though, that they would
all come to an end one day
That wall is starting to crumble, the protectors are trying
so hard not to back down
But they are exposing the ones they should protect, who
just lay crying on the ground

Bed

It's 3 O'clock in the morning, and I don't want
to go to bed
Cos once I lay my head down the noise starts
in my head
So I'm sat here tapping on the ipod
Writing useless shit instead

Words just seem to flow out, sometimes when I write
But most of it is probably just self-indulgent trite
Stop wallowing in your, whatever it is, and get
yourself a job
Feeling sorry for yourself won't stop you being
a benefit slob

We don't talk of hurt, we don't talk of pain
But we can talk about the weather, and has there
been much rain
If any D.I.Y needs doing we can give him a call
Cos he's been there and done it, he knows it all

But one enormous thing he misses, is his own
daughter's pain and hurt
Do I have to spell it out, write it across my shirt
Dad I've always needed you, I don't think that ever ends
Just some time, respect and space, could help a
broken heart to mend

Parents

Is it wrong to say bad things
About the people who gave me life
Because when they decided to have children
They stopped being just husband and wife

As a child I looked to them
To identify and meet my needs
Was it really my job
To always make them pleased?

Growing up is difficult
Somewhat of a minefield
This is made much harder
When your parents' deny your emotional needs

When a child is frightened
They reach out and look for help
They don't want to be ignored
Or tormented as they yelp

They just want you to hold them
Tell them it will be okay
Listen to their worries
Let them have their say

Provide them an environment
To let them be their self
Don't teach them to deny their feelings
To box them on a shelf

Whilst I know it's difficult to be a parent
Children don't come with any rules
Treat them with love, care and compassion
Don't use them as emotional tools

Listen to them

What can I do, to take the pain away
Cut myself, take pills, or box it away for another day
Or you could put pen to paper, let it flow out
through the ink
The words form sentences and poems, and once read,
make you think

Write it down, and read it out loud
Empty the box, remove the shroud
No-one you tell, thinks it was your fault
One day the truth will hit you like a lightning bolt

Listen to them when they tell you
You are strong, and you will get through
Neither are you evil, wrong or bad
And you're entitled to feel hurt, angry and sad

That night, it was not your fault, and you are
not to blame
Repetition of this concept will help dissolve the shame
So put your pen to paper, see it in black & white
You really weren't to blame Dawn, for what
happened that night

Dawn Pritchard

Poem

I wake up feeling disgust, guilt and shame

Like reliving that morning after again

Don't want to look at, or see myself

This really is messing with my mental health

Now I've disclosed and talked about it

The jigsaw pieces are beginning to fit

And the image I've feared for most of my life

Is real, not uncertain and it cuts like a knife

There's still a four letter word, I'm avoiding to say

But others have said it, maybe I'll say it one day

That word, it appears to be the key

So small, yet so powerful, say it and be free

It will always be a memory, living in my head

But maybe not so intrusive, that I wish I was dead

Acknowledge I was a victim, but a survivor I've become

I think that's where I'd like to be when all this work is
done

Transparency

Can you really see through me?

I feel as transparent as can be

Can you read my thoughts, my fears

Can you see I'm on the verge of tears

Can you read me like a book

With just one glance, one quick look

Can you see, the evil in me

The disgust, the shame, I know what you see

Don't look at me, because I know

My thoughts and fears are exposed and on show

It's like looking through a window pane

I know you can see the guilt the shame

What do you think that I see

When I see a reflection of me

I see what you do

Transparency lets the evil through

Dawn Pritchard

Jigsaw pieces

Look at the picture on the front of the box
See how the pieces all interlock
What do you do, when you can't make them fit
Even one at a time, bit by bit

What if the picture just doesn't make sense
Even after hours n hours, on this puzzle you've spent
So do you give up, and just walk away
Put it all back in the box, and try again another day

The picture on the box will still be the same
And the struggle to complete it, will always remain
But if you start with the corners, there's only
four of these
Then work on the border, the straight edges will
fit with ease

So now you've a foundation, a frame to work from
This will always be there, even if the middle
bit goes wrong
The rest of the pieces, may just seem like a jumbled pile
So sort them into smaller groups, this may take a while

If you follow this process, you will probably find
Parts of the picture will begin to make sense
in your mind
Each jigsaw piece is no good on its own
They need to be put together, for the whole picture
to be shown.

Windowsill

Sitting here on the windowsill

Lots of thinking and time to kill

Would I really like to jump

Land on the roof below in a lump

What if all I did was break a bone

Would I scream, would I moan

Was I hoping it would kill me outright

There'd be no more struggle, no more fight

Would that mean the battle's won

Or really only just begun

See no-one really knows, what happens when we die

Do our souls' really just float up into the sky?

Looking out the window, watching life go by

Should I really give up, not even try

They make it look so simple, the people down below

Time here really has no meaning, it just passes really
slow

Dawn Pritchard

Old Poems

I just read some old poems, they really make me sad
In some I sound quite crazy, I really must be mad
Looking out the window, wanting to jump or fall
Am I sane or insane, it's just too close to call

The feelings that run through them, still exist
inside of me
Have I really moved that far forward, is my
mind yet free?
Look towards the future, try let go of the past
Feelings and urges of self-harm, how long will they last?

Ward Round

He says I'll become dependant
If I stay here for too long
But what to do if staying here,
Helps to make me strong

It's like being caught
between the devil and the deep blue sea
I really do want to go home
I don't want another dependency

The past several days
really have been a new experience
opening up, disclosing, taking risks
and hoping it will all make sense

The vulnerability I feel
I hope will fade away
Because the body memories I'm having
Are really intense today

I feel so uncomfortable
In my own skin
I'm having thoughts of self-harm
And I don't want to give in

Staying here a little longer
Is really for the best
I'm trusting other people
I'm getting so much off my chest

Dawn Pritchard

Body Memories

Why today do I feel so shit?

I hate myself every bit

Keep feeling something is inside me

Pushing deep won't let me be

My body keeps remembering

Makes me uncomfortable, I'm struggling

I'd really like to just forget

Keep thinking, why aren't you over it yet?

I feel embarrassment and shame

Now I've disclosed, never feel the same

Feel like all eyes can see through me

Can see my vulnerability

Yesterday I bought razor blades

To terminate, not to injure I'm afraid

But, I didn't use them I handed them in

Then the frustration and anger started to begin

Leave Cancelled

I want to say I'm sorry

For the disappointment and worry I have caused

I never meant to hurt you

Or spoil what we had planned to do

The emotions just took over

They consume me from within

I lose all control and focus

And everything tumbles down

I feel so confused and frightened

And panic starts to set in

You must believe me when I say

I want all this to change

I don't want to hurt anymore

And I don't want to cause you pain

I want to become a whole person

I want to live life again

Dad

If we were to have a conversation
What would I want to say?
I would ask, why you abandoned me
Was it because I'm gay?

Do you feel I let you down?
Have I brought you shame?
You know you have two daughters
But you don't treat us the same

Do you know you were my hero
I looked up to you so much
All I wanted, was to please you
But you still don't get in touch

I moved two hundred miles away
Mum said, it would be for the best
Easier for you to get your head around
My being gay, it's true I do not jest

So if we were to have a conversation
That's what I would say, Dad.

Poem

If I knew what I was feeling

I'd try to write it down

If I knew what I was feeling

I'd wear it like a crown

You see my head, it really is blank

And it's not just the skunk I have to thank

Denial, detachment they're here too

Who should we listen to, what should we do?

Like the proverbial rabbit caught in the headlight

The choice is simple really, either fight or flight

Which should I pick, I really don't know

So being the coward I am, I'm giving flying a go

Is it really wrong to want to prevent the pain?

Cos it tears me up inside and drives me insane

So if flying means hiding away

Then that's what we'll do today

Dialectic Behavioural Therapy

What can I write?

What should I write?

Is what I'm writing a load of shite?

Snippets of moments, that make up my day

Don't ask me to identify, cos it's too hard to say

You want to write about feelings, I've never

done this before

You see my emotional literacy really is quite poor

So if I write it like this, it doesn't feel as real

A kind of protective bubble that DBT is trying to steal

Meditation, relaxation, mindfulness with a horse

Wise, emotional and reasonable mind, stick with

the Emo Reg course

So what can I write?

What should I write?

Is what I'm writing a load of shite?

Poem

My parents still aren't talking to me
They've sent my nana home to die
I just want to curl up in a corner
And let myself cry

But you see I have a problem
I don't know how to let go
So we plant the emotions in a box
And watch the roots of guilt and judgement grow

It's like standing on a beach
Waiting for the tidal wave to hit
I can see it coming towards me
But I can't get out of the sand pit

The wave washes over me
And knocks me to the ground
I lay lifeless on the sand
Waiting to be found

A second wave is coming
And I try to make a stand
But it drags my body out to sea
Away from the safety of land

Dawn Pritchard

I try to fight against the waves
And get back to the shore
But the current's intense and the waves are strong
They shake me to my core

I splutter to the surface
And try to catch my breath
A part of me has given up already
And is hoping for imminent death

What is this therapy?

Emotions, what the fuck are they
Floating through your head night and day
Waiting to pounce and trip you up
They take over your day, like a cloud of bad luck

Emotions apparently are different to thoughts
Don't mix them up that's how I got caught
I've been told that, just cos you thought it,
don't make it so
Got to keep emotions n thoughts separate whilst
giving DBT a go

Mindfulness is the way forward, to inner peace and calm
A journey of discovery, a move away from self-harm
But what about the questions, that keep floating
through my head
And the thoughts of going to the travel lodge, and
seeing myself dead

Then we come to Marsha, with her bob
and Deirdre Barlow specs!
Are you sure this woman's genuine, did anyone
do a CRB check?
I mean, one minute she says think of that, and the
next think of this
I'm not a bloody robot, don't take the piss

Dawn Pritchard

Our Teddy Bear

The ink just flows from the pen
Recalling memories, of a time when
We were not listened to
Or really shown what to do

If we were hurt, or just unsure
We weren't encouraged or shown the score
We were left to drown in our fears
Sat alone to mop our tears

Cuddles is our teddy bear
We'd hold him tight, we knew he cared
Sometimes with him, we'd cry to sleep
Knowing our secrets he would keep

25 years on, we still have Cuddles
We squeeze him tight when our mind is muddled
What would he say, if he could speak?
Would he divulge that we feel like a freak?

Poem

Why am I sitting here feeling sad?

I'm out of hospital I should be glad

I just want to go back to bed

Stop the self-harm thoughts in my head

Cut my wrists, watch them bleed

Would that really make me pleased?

Don't know if it's about punishment or pain

What would I lose? What would I gain?

More scars to look at, on my arms

Does it make me feel better, make me calm?

But makes others stress and cause worry

Back to hospital in a hurry

Is hospital where I want to be?

Not even sure any more, what's wrong with me

Even though I'm under CATT

Don't feel like talking, just feel flat

Poem

Wait until she falls asleep, then go off in the car

Find somewhere quiet, not necessarily too far

All I need to take is a sharp blade and meds

A part of me feels, I'd be better off dead

Drift away peacefully, no chaos just calm

To take ones' own life, the ultimate self-harm

No more fear or panic, like I'm losing my mind

Just slip away quietly, where no-one will find

If I leave letters of apology, will it just cause more pain

What I write won't really matter, they'll just think

I'm insane

How do you tell people, you don't want to live anymore

Because everything hurts, and just feels so raw

What do you see?

Look at the circle, what do you see?

A continuous battle or a chance to break free

Keep rolling it forward just like a ball

Maintain the momentum, so you don't fall

The journey may be long, with bumps on the way

But on top of the ball you really must stay

The ball may bounce high, but it will also come down

So don't let that smile turn into a frown

Keeping on top of things can be tough

Especially when you feel like you've really had enough

Talking can be helpful, it's good to let things go

Learning to identify feelings and let emotions show

Poem

Does feeling numb mean the process has begun?

Sorting through emotions and feelings really isn't fun

Hold on to the thought that this will make us strong

That's what everyone says, they can't all be wrong

Sleeping all the time, is the safest thing to do

Don't focus on self-harm, let the thoughts just pass
through

Over medicate myself, we know it induces sleep

Helps dissolve the secrets we no longer want to keep

Aunty Jacqui

I wish I had the words to say
How much I have been dreading this day
I can't believe it is one year on
It's even harder to accept that she's gone

Memories of her flood my mind
But words of comfort I cannot find
Talking about her in past tense
Just does not make any sense

'Our Dawn' is what she called me
Always happy for me just to be
She never judged, she never teased
Was only ever really pleased

You are what you are, is what she'd say
Never an issue my being gay
Singing and dancing, nights out on the town
Always smiling and laughing, never a frown

These memories of you, in my mind I'll keep
They trigger dreams, when I sleep
Of happy times when you were here
But now you're gone, and we shed our tears

CATT

I tend to write a ditty

Especially when I'm feeling shitty

But I just wanted to say

That CATT stepped in and saved the day

Always on the end of the phone

You've helped when I'm feeling alone

Your patience, support and care

Has helped me open up and share

The work that you guys do

Has really pulled me through

I know your job is hard

So I thought I'd say thank you with this card

Have your say

C'mon you have so much to say
Why so fucking quiet today
You claim you've never had a voice
This is your time stand up make a choice

I thought you wanted the world to see
That you're the little girl in me
So come on up and have your say
Don't be afraid, tell them in your own way

We know all the crying makes you feel bad
But your experiences have actually been quite sad
So go on, just let the tears flow
I know it hurts and the process is slow

We tried to look after you and keep you
hidden from view
We didn't know how else we were supposed
to protect you
And now we're being told to just let you
scream and shout
But a blade would be better, just cut it out.

Dawn Pritchard

Feeling Lost

Feeling lost and so confused

Look at your choices, which will you choose

Trying so hard to keep us from harm

Denial has been great, worked like a charm

Can't go back now, the words they're out

Whether we whisper them quietly or scream and shout

Got to just go with the flow

Step by step nice and slow

Feelings are raging from A to Z

Tying me up, I can't break free

Try keep it together, don't dare let go

Cos the feelings will devour you and emotions will show.

Need to grieve

They tell me that I need to grieve

For those who weren't listened to or believed

The ones who were hurt and lived within

Who feel as though they've committed some sin

Where do I start, where do I begin

How to let the feelings out from within

I start to cry not knowing why

Just to sit with them I really try

When someone dies you know the pain

But this just does not seem the same

I try to give it, its rightful name

But all I end up feeling is guilt and shame

Embarrassed by what I feel I did wrong

I feel so weak, not big and strong

The therapy I'm going through

Will hopefully help uncover the real you

Dawn Pritchard

What's going on?

What the hell is going on?

Pritchard women are supposed to be strong

You are weak and not much use

So find a tree and tie a noose

Hold on a minute, not so fast

It's time to believe in you at last

Give yourself a little break

You're not invisible nor a fake

It's there loss they don't see you

You've only ever been honest, open and true

So don't worry if you falter, it's your time

Just dust yourself off, you'll be just fine

A, physical armour is not what you need

Nor a white knight upon his steed

Just have the confidence to look within

Your future is there, waiting to begin

Wronged you

What have I done that's wronged you so much?

That you don't contact me or keep in touch

Are my problems too much for you to take?

How do you think that makes me feel for fuck sake?

I've done no wrong that I know

But care for me you just don't show

On my own is how I feel

Moments of belonging I try to steal

What can I do to make you see?

That I need your support to help set me free

My past haunts me all day long

It takes all my energy to remain strong

A call, a text, is all I need

To stop me wanting to make myself bleed

When I hurt myself it's because I'm in pain

I just want to feel like I'm part of a family again

Poem

How am I supposed to give Pebbles a voice?

Things happened to her, of which she had no choice

She is so badly hurt I don't know where to start

The horse has already bolted, and she was left pulling the cart

We kept her hidden to protect her you see

But part of her is already dead, between you and me

The pain is difficult and intense to bear

We could just kill her, no one would care

They row all the time inside my head

Just scream and shout, I'm sure we'd be better dead

They don't listen when I ask them to stop

They start with no warning, catch me on the hop

Try to sit quietly, relax and stay calm

Don't listen to Fred when he says let's self-harm

Just give Pebbles the chance to have her say

Then she'll retreat back to her den to hide away

Nana & Grandad

Every now and then the thought pops in my head
I'm never gonna see them again, they really are dead
I keep looking at the box, with grandad's dvd
I want to watch it again but am scared the emotions
will break free

You see it really is too devastating to try to accept
But Lord and Lady Swillington I will not forget
I wish that I could see them just to say hello
To tell them that I love them and didn't want them to go

They were both such amazing people, they gave such
happiness to so many
Had such a huge family, never met another so
large, not any
They had 15 children, 10 boys and 5 girls,
grand children they had 41
And the great-great grandkids started arriving
one by one

67 years together, once got an anniversary
card from the Queen
A more loving and wonderful couple I have never seen
I know I'm not alone, with the sentiments when I say
I love and miss you both dearly every single day

Dawn Pritchard

Where we met

People sometimes ask me, where I met my other half
Now there's a funny story, are you ready for a laugh?
We met on a psychiatric ward, over at Chase Farm
She was there for depression, me too, but
also self-harm

We'd have chats in the smoking room, at first I didn't
know she was gay
Then she talked about her ex-girlfriend one
particular day
I really liked her as a friend, and to be honest didn't
think I stood a chance
She was funny, gorgeous and fit, she wouldn't give
me a second glance

I was soon discharged, and back to my flat I went
She was still in hospital and needed a friend to vent
So I'd meet her, listen to her venting, but I
didn't say a word
I couldn't tell her that I fancied her that would be absurd

Then one day I plucked up the courage, and
told her how I felt
She said she felt the same, and all my worries
began to melt
We became an item, and I moved into her flat
Ten years later we're still together, living with
our 3 crazy cats

I am a hoarder

Last night I watched a show about a woman
who hoards stuff
She couldn't get rid of anything, throwing things away
was just too tough
I could see this woman's struggle, I could
clearly see her pain
Most of her attempts to change her situation
really were in vain.

Now whilst I don't hoard objects around me, I
hoard stuff in my head
Emotions, feelings and memories are stored
in there instead
Trying to clear them out is no easy task, the
layers are so many
And the skills I need to do it, I don't feel I have any

Now the therapist told this woman, her hoarding was
connected to a trauma
And until she dealt with this, she'd continue to be caught
up in this drama
She really was reluctant to delve into her past
Using humour as a defence, then closing
down really fast

At this point I found myself crying, and not
being aware of why
So I covered my face with my hand to cover up my eyes

But les saw and ask what's wrong, why are you upset?
I said I didn't know, i'm just stupid, don't worry
pass me a cigarette

You see if I don't know why I'm emotional, if I can't justify
why I'm crying
Then I must pull the shutters down and go
back into hiding
Each layer is full of pain and hurt, its built up n up
over the years
So I hoarded the emotions, feelings and memories and
created a reservoir of tears

Every now and then the reservoir bursts its banks
And the tears start flowing, and sadness rumbles in the
background like a tank
Sometimes this turns to anger n it eats me up inside
Makes me feel bad, want to hurt myself, run
away n hide

So I too am a hoarder, hoarding things inside my head
Wondering whether I'll ever have the courage to face up
to the dread
I really am, scared to trust, that letting go is a must
Cos once it's out you can't go back, and I fear
that I will combust

Sectioned

Back in 2004 my mind was confused and unsure
I thought I was getting messages from
the satellite next door
Feelings of omnipotence and quite a bit of weed too
And that's how I ended up in hospital on a Section 2

At a meeting with my shrink, he said I want you
to come in for a while
I looked at him and then my keyworker and
I began to smile
He never wants me in hospital, this is some kind of joke
But, no he wasn't joking, confidentiality
soon to be revoked

Now when the second doctor saw me he
agreed with my shrink
Didn't need to look twice or take long to think
I agree with your doctor he said, put her on section 2
So it was off quick to the ward, no please or thank you

The nurses were surprised that I was so calm
And that I had arrived having not self-harmed
You see some of my informal admissions of the past
Had meant calming me down, and that could be
quite a task

You see I didn't think my shrink would really Section me
So my calmness was a gamble that I would
soon be free
But it didn't pay off because the ASW agreed too
Saying we are going to keep you here for up
to 28 days under Section 2

www.ingramcontent.com/pod-product-compliance
Lightning Source LLC
Chambersburg PA
CBHW031220290326
41931CB00035B/624